DIVINELY
Courageous

ISBN (eBook/Kindle): 979-8-90379-952-7

ISBN (Paperback): 979-8-90379-953-4

ISBN (Hardcover): 979-8-90379-954-1

Library Of Congress Catalog Card Number: Applied

Published in the United States of America by Lynx Publishers.

DIVINELY
Courageous

NINA AUSTIN

Dedication

I dedicate this book with utmost love and respect to my husband Jack who has been a constant source of encouragement and inspiration.

Table of Contents

Part 1.
The Spiritual Transformation From Fear to Faith

Chapter 1

There are days when life on earth feels like we have spent a few moments stuck on a roller coaster. Now imagine yourself holding on tight for dear life! Maybe you are wondering if you should be afraid or look for some humor in this scenario. Life definitely comes with its ups and downs! Most everything depends on our perception of life and what's going on within ourselves, and in the world around us.

Life can bring an abundance of happiness and laughter, but we know it can also be very difficult. How do we find equal balance so that all of life's problems don't prevent us from embracing joy and serenity?

A somber reality of life is that listening to a few moments of the news can leave us with a feeling of sadness. When we think we have heard the absolute worst possible scenario, we can be fairly certain there is another horrific event soon to follow.

The injustice in these violent actions can bring out many of our human emotions. Not only sadness, but at times anger at these senseless acts resulting in loss of lives and physical suffering. These emotions can also lead to a feeling of fear or hopelessness.

It's a common occurrence that when these things happen, we hear expressions of sympathy like "thoughts and prayers" for the unfortunate victims and their families. Then, as time passes, and the news media are finished covering the latest tragedy, it's politics as usual. Life goes on.

As heartbreaking as it is, it has become part of life as we know it. We can't bury our heads in the sand or turn a deaf ear to what's going on in the world. I imagine there are some who do, but realistically, most of us don't. Even if we choose to limit our time spent listening to the news, it is usually passed on to us through family or friends. It's inescapable.

I think perhaps sometimes God gives the hardest battles to his strongest warriors. Other times, he gives his weakest warriors the hardest battles, so we will look to him to find our strength.

Life is for the living, so we carry on with hope of making the world a better place. How do we find joy and peace amidst the chaos?

There is always a light at the end of the tunnel. It may appear dim at first, and at times we don't always see the light, but if we persevere and follow this light, we can find peace and serenity. Despite all that's taking place all over the world, we are meant to experience love and joy! Jesus has proclaimed he is the Light of the World! *(John 8:12)*

Once we acknowledge our fears, we can learn to overcome them so we can find peace and encourage others to find peace and harmony in their lives!

We were given our lives to be of service to God and help one another. God did not bless us with the miracle of our lives to live merely for ourselves, but to use our spiritual gifts to encourage others by sharing our faith and hope. When our intentions are a reflection of our personal relationship with God, we can be assured that it comes from a place of selfless love.

As divided as we are, as a nation and a world, our creator sees and loves each one of us as the cherished children of his creation. We are meant to love and help one another, but our fears have separated us. We fail to see one another as God sees us.

God has not given us a spirit of fear. He has given us a spirit of power and love and a sound mind. *(2 Timothy 1:7 ESV)*

Fear is the unwelcome intruder that can be disguised in many forms. Sometimes it's found in the obvious, and other times it is buried deep inside of us, and it becomes a part of our emotional and mental psyche.

Fear can be debilitating and keep us from embracing our full potential. It can also cause us to distance ourselves from others. It isn't always easy to acknowledge fear. Many times, that is attributed to our pride and ego.

The first time I was willing to be honest about my fears, it felt like a heavy weight was no longer mine to carry. Fear could no longer steal my joy or have a grip on my emotions. I felt hopeful and free.

To try to make sense of the troubling times we live in, we can turn to God, read His Word in Scripture, and hit our knees in prayer. We can plead with God for His Divine intervention, but can we still hold on to hope that all these horrific events taking place all around us will stop, or at least become less frequent? For that matter, will our own personal fears ever be put to rest?

Once we acknowledge our fears and have the willingness to admit to them, our spiritual transformation brings us to the point of acceptance. We accept that we need God in every aspect of our lives. The wisdom of God is incomprehensible to us. Reliance and trust in him give us confidence and the strength to persevere through faith.

Acquiring faith is a lifelong process. We don't have to be bursting at the seams in our faith journey. God has told us in Scripture that all we need is the faith of a mustard seed. (*Matthew 17:20 ESV*)

In our quest for faith, we begin to feel calm and experience quiet moments of gratitude. We may begin to feel like we have been awakened from a long slumber and feel renewed and hopeful! These spiritual awakenings are part of God's plan for us. They happen more frequently when we put God first in our lives. This is the peace of God that surpasses all human understanding! (*Philippians 4:7 ESV*)

To find acceptance, accompanied by God's grace, brings the courage to live a life free from continuous worry and all the challenges of life that can weigh us down. We can find freedom, peace, and gentleness in God's Spirit.

Sometimes we are busy living, and fear never crosses our minds. So many emotions are at rest until we find ourselves personally affected, and fear can catch us off guard and hit us like a ton of bricks. Serious illness, a loss of financial stability, divorce, and an endless list of unexpected circumstances can creep up on us.

How do we wage our own personal battle with this potentially paralyzing emotion?

Chapter 2

Let's start by bringing to light some of the most common fears we experience. Even though our sometimes egotistical selves want to deny ownership of a fear, it still exists. For some, it is camouflaged by unhealthy coping skills, such as relying on alcohol or drugs that produce a false sense of security and well-being.

I recently listened to a sermon in which the pastor spoke about fear. He shared that in his experience, the number one fear people have is the fear of public speaking. The second is the fear of dying. If that's an accurate assessment, then you can find humor when you imagine someone who is more fearful of honoring someone's life by delivering their eulogy than the fear of dying themselves! Is their fear that great that they would rather trade places with the deceased? Unless that truly is their greatest fear, I seriously doubt that!

Since most of us aren't called on a regular basis to be public speakers, I believe that at the top of the list of fears is the fear of our death or the death of a loved one.

There are those among us who have found acceptance and a feeling of peace through developing a personal relationship with our Creator. Their freedom from fear is based on faith, hope, and trust.

Others continue to struggle with the inevitable. That doesn't indicate a complete lack of faith. Even though fear and faith cannot co-exist, we are all in different places in our faith journey! If we're willing to be honest, we all have fears. It's the methods we use to cope with our fears that may differ.

There are unanswered questions that can come to mind when the thought of our death or the death of a loved one passes through our minds. Many would prefer to put this fear aside and allow it to remain safely hidden in the darkest crevices of the mind. After all, it isn't considered a favorite topic for conversation at Sunday dinner at Grandma's house, or in our personal discussions with family and friends. It normally doesn't result in an upbeat, cheerful conversation!

I believe it's important to have these sometimes uncomfortable discussions with our families and those we hold close to our hearts.

We often make assumptions that our loved ones are doing okay when actually they are in need of our love, care, and encouragement. For our aging loved ones, a lot of emphasis is placed on their physical health, which is normally our number one concern. Their emotional and spiritual health is equally important for their overall well-being.

For aging parents with dementia and other diseases of the brain, it may not be possible to communicate effectively with them. To be patient and understanding, under such difficult circumstances, is the most effective way to show them love.

Engaging in conversation with those near and dear to us gives us the opportunity to ask how they feel about life and death. Taking the time to listen to their response is a form of love. They may inspire us, or maybe they are feeling some fear, and it helps them to talk openly about their feelings and to know they are not alone. I don't believe we should assume that because they have faith, they are eagerly awaiting the afterlife and don't have some questions and concerns. We are all children of our loving God and should be approached with love and tender compassion.

Christ himself had a question when he sacrificed his own life for us. He cried out, "My God, my God, why have you forsaken me?"

It isn't always the things we say, but the things we don't say that are important. These conversations can bring our loved ones hope and encouragement. If they are strong in faith, this also gives them the opportunity to share their faith and feel as though they are actively participating in life. It gives them the opportunity to return our love and encourage us in our own faith journey.

We get frequent reminders that so many young people lose their lives unexpectedly through unforeseen circumstances. We usually consider age as the determining factor as to how long we will live, but so many can attest to the fact that this doesn't always hold true!

Some of the concerns we have regarding the end-of-life passage can be difficult to process until we are able to reach acceptance. The answers lie in those questions that have no guaranteed answers. We don't know if our loved ones or we will suffer any physical pain of death, or if we will leave this earth unexpectedly. Perhaps we may fall asleep and pass peacefully, and our fears may never come to fruition. This is our hope.

I received a sympathy card following the loss of a loved one that I found very comforting. The verse compares death to an unborn baby in its mother's womb. If a baby could speak and were asked if they wanted to leave their familiar surroundings, most likely they would say no. They have no awareness of what awaits them when they're born. They haven't experienced the joys or challenges of living.

The same as passing from life to death. We are often reluctant to leave this earth for the same reason. We feel comfortable with the only life we have ever known. When we experience life on earth, it prepares us, through God's Word, to anticipate everlasting life. The expression "don't be a baby" takes on a different meaning if we choose to look at it from this perspective!

Is it humanly possible to find enough courage to conquer those fears in both life and the process of death? The fears that often leave us in a state of denial, and we are unable to verbally acknowledge them?

Chapter 3

Fear takes residence in the uncertainties of life. It's comprised of all the "what if's" and the "what ifs not" of everyday living.

Another acknowledged fear that can rank at the top of the list of frightful experiences is flying. Some relax and enjoy the flight, and others breathe a sigh of relief when the plane arrives safely on the runway. We often find laughter when we readily admit our fear is not of flying, it's the fear of crashing! Flying also correlates with the sense of losing control. As part of our human nature, the inability to control situations can be so invasive that it leaves one feeling helpless, which can result in self-induced panic. We find ourselves hitching a ride on the fear coaster again, holding on tight and hoping it will pass quickly. I personally do not prefer to fly. Beginning with long lines and flight delays, combined with turbulence during the fight, it isn't a favorite thing I enjoy doing. If you ever see a woman doing the happy dance as she exits the airplane, that would be me. Each time declaring, "I am never doing that again!" I highly recommend you pray before the flight and not during. It's impossible to have faith and fear at the same time! From my personal experience, I feel much calmer when I pray before I board the flight!

Franklin D Roosevelt brought out a human reaction to fear in his inaugural address in 1934. He proclaimed, "We have nothing to fear but fear itself." There is logic to this statement, but the "spiritual" truth about fear is based on God's messages to us in Scripture. No words are as meaningful and as important as the Word of God.

Oftentimes, we find ourselves with a laundry list of fears that can be quite overwhelming. Fear of failure, loss of a job, and anticipation of economic insecurity. Fear of rejection, worrying about our spouses, our children, and all those we hold close at heart.

Our desire to take control of our lives and often trying to intervene in the lives of our loved ones can leave us feeling frustrated and with a sense of helplessness. If not acknowledged, we continue to add to that laundry list of anxiety and fear, and it begins to pile up.

Is it possible to live a worry-free life, free of doubt, fear, and the insecurities that can cause us to lose hope?

We may never entirely conquer all of our fears, but in the process of trying, we can find peace of mind so that we aren't holding ourselves hostage to worrisome thoughts.

This may sound discouraging because we usually prefer to find immediate solutions for whatever problems we face. In my daily walk with God, I have realized I need to be patient. Everything in God's time and not our time.

If we focus on the everlasting love of Christ, we become less fearful, and our faith will guide us into the light of God's grace. Within his grace, our hope in him will sustain us and help us to trust that no matter what life throws our way, his love and protection will always prevail.

We can't control the world around us, but within God's love and mercy, we find the gift of faith, our saving grace. The divine intervention that can change our lives and help us to turn all of our fear, worry, and anxiety over to the all-encompassing hands of our loving, all-knowing God.

For most of us, our first experience with the "fear factor" came as a child. Take a moment to reflect on your first memory of a fear you experienced as a child. No matter how unpleasant that memory is, you are a survivor! Any fears you have encountered up to this point in your life, you have survived for a reason. Whether it was the encouragement of a parent or parental figure, your own determination to be brave, or a leap of faith, your personal experiences have led you into the present moment.

All of our past, present, and future experiences are a part of God's plan for us. They don't always make sense to us, and many things will remain a mystery until the day when God will reveal himself to us, complete in all of his glory, and there will be no more unanswered questions. Total peace comes without questions!

My first childhood memory of feeling afraid occurred one evening as I was laying on the floor in the living room doing my homework. I could hear the sound of the nightly news in the background. I glanced up and saw a man on TV shaking his fist as he declared, "We will bury you!" A monster in a child's eyes. His name was Nikita Khrushchev, ruler and dictator of the Union of Soviet Socialist Republics.

I immediately felt a wave of anxiety, and I sat up and looked to my father for comfort. He calmed my fears and assured me he was just another bully threatening to destroy our nation, but would not succeed. I had nothing to fear. I felt much calmer and had the reassurance that everything would be okay, simply because he said so! The unquestioning trust of a "childlike" faith!

Chapter 4

Our Heavenly Father waits for us to bring our fears to him. His love for all of us is divinely different than the love we have for one another. God's love for us cannot be changed. Nothing we do can make him love us more or love us less. The everlasting love of God is one of our most profound blessings.

When he created us, he knew that we would have fears. In fact, "fear or fear not" is mentioned over three hundred times in Scripture. He did not leave us here on earth defenseless against fearful situations. He had all bases covered, so we could stand strong in faith and have the courage that faith in him brings.

One of the most well-known Scripture Verses that brings me comfort is found in *Isaiah 41:10 ESV*.

Fear not, for I am with you;

Be not dismayed, for I am your God.

I will strengthen you,

Yes, I will help you,

I will uphold you with My righteous right hand.

God's Word comforts us, reassures us, and fills our minds and hearts with love and hope in him! Without God's promises to us, hope in him would fail to exist. We would coast through life with no defense against Satan, the enemy who desires to destroy us. When we are living in a constant state of fear, he rejoices. It brings him great pleasure when he believes he holds the power to destroy our souls, and cause us to turn away from the one whose love for us began even before he created us! The love that, when we turn to him, cannot be defeated by evil.

With God's steadfast love and our acceptance of his saving grace, we find our protection in him when we make the choice to follow him.

Matthew 16:24

Take Up Your Cross and Follow Jesus

24 Then Jesus told his disciples, "If anyone would come after me, let him deny himself and take up his cross and follow me.

Chapter 5

For Christians, the most powerful love was Christ's sacrificial death on the Cross. The ultimate and perfect love for mankind. There will never be any greater, more passionate, and divinely courageous love than his!

To conquer our fears, God has given us direct means of connecting and communicating with him. For many of us taking a walk in nature brings us calm and the peaceful awareness of being close to him. When we rejoice in his creation, we find joy in all that he has done, and his Spirit walks with us.

When I meditate, I take deep breaths, and focus on things that bring calm and happiness. I like to visualize the gentle ripple of the waves and the different shades of blue in the ocean, or the vivid colors of nature. So many gifts of God's creation are calming to the mind and cast out fear.

When we talk to God through prayer, his Spirit is alive in us and we feel a perfect peace that puts our fears to rest. The peaceful feeling that we receive when we place ourselves in the glory of his presence.

In Scripture, God speaks to us about prayer. The following Scripture verses are what I think of as his love letters to all of us.

Philippians 4:6-7

6 Do not be anxious about anything, but in everything by prayer and supplication with thanksgiving let your requests be made known to God.

7 And the peace of God, which surpasses all understanding, will guard your hearts and your minds in Christ Jesus.

In the next passage from Scripture we can sense God's deep love for us as expressed in his "groaning." Groaning indicates a deep sense of passion and love, that exceeds the physical pain that we associate with the word "groaning."

Romans 8:26

26 Likewise the Spirit helps us in our weakness. For we do not know what to pray for as we ought, but the Spirit himself intercedes for us with groaning too deep for words.

Chapter 6

Through God's grace, He gives us other ways to be of service to him. Trusting God helps to diminish our own worries and concerns and equips us to help others in the process.

Our father has commanded us to love one another. Through God's Infinite love and our love for others, we are able to lift one another up and act as his disciples.

John 13:34-35(ESV)

34 A new commandment I give to you, that you love one another: just as I have loved you, you also are to love one another.

35 By this all people will know that you are my disciples, if you have love for one another."

If we fully embrace the true meaning of God's love, which is pure and selfless love, we have the opportunity to reach out to others and share our hope. This is a priceless gift we receive when we call out to him. Through loving others, we can offer them hope, encouragement, and the assurance that they also can find freedom from living with constant negative and hopeless feelings.

This Scripture verse is uplifting to the soul and speaks of the joy that hope brings. It also reassures us that God hears our prayers!

Romans 12:12

12 Rejoice in hope, be patient in tribulation, be constant in prayer.

God promised never to abandon us. He didn't just leave us here on earth to figure things out on our own. He not only gave us the assurance of his Word and the means to communicate with him, but he gave us the gift of one another.

Chapter 7

In a recent conversation with a friend, she commented that she had no fear. I found her comment interesting and thought-provoking to say the least. I began to doubt her sincerity. Is it possible that in our humanness, we have no fear? If we had no fear of anything, would we even need God?

Her answer was inspiring, and she said that at that moment in time, she felt no fear because she felt the Spirit of God working within her and through her.

God speaks to us through others. Other times, he speaks through you and me, to reach out to others to show the courage and love that comes when we are filled with his loving, nurturing Spirit. The heart of his Spirit dwells within us and among us if we open our hearts to receive it.

The presence of the Holy Spirit is what our souls long for and desperately need. We tend to think of God as being in heaven, or somewhere in the sky, or some distant place until we see him face to face. The realization that he is right here with us brings us a beautiful feeling of peace and comfort. When we believe this to be true, it draws us close to him. It aligns our hearts with his and leads us to the serenity that brings us comfort and joy. It sets us free from any fearful thoughts that come to our minds, which only add fuel to our anxiety and worries.

Fear can come in waves, and it isn't always the major things we fear. Sometimes we fear the judgment of others. People pleasing is a byproduct of fear, seeking the approval of others. Am I good enough, or do I measure up? What do others think of me?

An example of suffering from different types of fear and anguish is social anxiety. This is very difficult for the afflicted to cope with. This is a form of fear that can be difficult to face alone. The desperate feeling of wanting to avoid large crowds, hoping for an immediate escape route to help them return to their comfort zone. They can't seem to escape quickly enough.

The post-COVID pandemic has been added to the list of fears for some, who are still reluctant to take part in large public gatherings. There are some who were traumatized by the Coronavirus. Although it wasn't the first time the world faced a plague, we were all in uncharted waters. Fear spread rapidly. The fear was spreading more rapidly than the virus!

There are many among us who suffer from PTSD and can become paralyzed with fear. The human mind doesn't have a delete option, capable of erasing terrifying memories. In cases of extreme fear, counseling or a spiritual mentor may help. To be able to share those painful memories helps them to know they are loved and supported. Each time they share their memories, they are one step further in their healing process.

Setting unrealistic expectations of others can also bring on fear of disappointment. This can cause us to harbor resentments towards one another. This type of fear can cause disappointment that leads to conflict.

Many can become fearful of standing strong in their convictions because there are those who are so easily offended. They aren't always tender-hearted, sensitive beings with easily hurt feelings. They may or may not realize they are actually claiming various injustices by attempting to bully others into submission.

If we are going to follow Christ, regardless of all these issues, then situations like this require love and tolerance. Christ never said it would be easy!

If we allow ourselves to get too caught up in what's wrong with the world, we are destined to fail to love one another as Christ has commanded us to do!

That doesn't mean we have to agree to the ways of the world, but we are not to "conform" to the ways of the world either.

Romans 12:2

Do not be conformed to this world, but be transformed by the renewal of your mind, that by testing you may discern what is the will of God, what is good and acceptable and perfect.

Chapter 8

When we seek a solution to life's personal struggles, no matter whether we seek spiritual counseling, read God's Word in Scripture, or pour our hearts out to him in prayer, God is always with us in Spirit, wanting us to look to him for help and turn away from the dangers of this world.

Communion with God through prayer each day keeps us close to him. We have all been given this opportunity to grow in faith.

I participated in a sermon series entitled "The School of Prayer." At the beginning of the series, I found myself changing my perception of prayer.

It was suggested that there were more effective ways to pray that would bring us close to God in a more meaningful, reverent way. Were my prayers not between myself and God and a part of my personal relationship with him? Wasn't the fact that I was even praying at all a good thing?

After giving it more thought, I was able to look at prayer differently. I learned that the most pleasing prayers to God are when I begin by praising him and thanking him for all of my blessings, asking for his forgiveness, and then placing my prayer requests before him.

It was also brought to light that at this point, most of us start listing all of our God, "please do or please do not dos." I could definitely relate to that!. It's as if we are telling God what we think he should do! Our infinite God of wisdom already knows what to do! Prayer is our personal connection to God. Anyone can pray in whichever way they choose. This was only my personal learning experience.

This form of communication made with God made sense to me. I found that remembering these things was helpful to me, and I felt like my communication with him changed and would continue to give me the means to use prayer to strengthen my relationship with him.

It's sometimes challenging to effectively communicate with others. A difficult-to-relate-to co-worker, perhaps a family member we may butt heads with, or even a complete stranger that we find difficult to deal with. Communication with God also helps us to communicate with others more effectively.

If I am praying for healing for a sick family member or a friend, or if I have been asked to pray for someone I have never met, I have found myself becoming more aware of the words He has given us, "In The Lord's Prayer, Thy will be done." I can't bargain with or try to manipulate God! I know God's will be done, whether I am willing to accept it or not! That is a constant reminder to me that I need to pray for acceptance.

I became aware that many times my prayers were like a one-sided conversation, with me doing all the talking! I have to continue to learn to be still and wait patiently for God's answer to my prayers. This calls to mind the Scripture verse *"Be still and know that I am God!" **(Psalm 46:10 ESV)***

It was also emphasized in this series that the most important aspect of prayer is not just asking God for what we hope he will do. It's how we form our personal relationship with him in a way that brings Honor, Glory and Reverence to his Holy Name.

Chapter 9

No matter what fear we are confronted with, God hears our prayers and cries for help. His desire for us is to seek his Spirit so he can console us and grant us his peace! That peace that surpasses all human understanding. It's not possible to fully understand the Supreme nature of God!

When it comes to our relationship with God, I try to avoid "overthinking." I have recalled a friend humorously referring to overthinking as analysis paralysis! Trying to understand all of God's wondrous ways could definitely bring us to that point!

This Scripture verse is also another reminder to trust God and not frustrate ourselves by trying to figure everything out by relying on our limited human intellect.

Proverbs 3:5-6

5 Trust in the Lord with all your heart, and do not lean on your own understanding.

6 In all your ways acknowledge him, and he will make straight your paths.

Theologians and Spiritual Mentors have dedicated themselves to studying the Scriptures so we are not misinterpreting the Word of

God. There has been ongoing controversy for centuries, and they often disagree, and most likely they always will. I believe God reveals to us exactly what he feels we are able to comprehend and what we need to know to be of service to him.

Our awesome God did not create us to spend our lives crippled by confusion. When the Spirit of God is within us, our heavenly Father is our source of wisdom and truth.

Chapter 10

Turning our lives over to the care of God is an ongoing process. It requires surrendering to him, trusting him, and developing patience and persistence. It is a lifetime effort and requires discipline and obedience to his commands in Scripture. Since we are all sinners, if we acknowledge our sins before God and repent for them, then we are forgiven. His glorious Resurrection preceded by his excruciating pain on the cross made this possible for us. He came to save and change the world. Unfortunately, at times we can try to sugarcoat the Word of God to justify our sins. God sees our hearts and through his grace, and our awareness that we need to be honest with ourselves, we can live according to his Word. We are all God's children and have a sinful nature. This reminds me of his Words to us in Scripture when he said,

Matthew 7:-3 ESV

"Whoever trusts in his own heart is a fool, but he who walks in wisdom will be delivered"

I remember years ago, I would give a coworker rides to work. She was much older than me and she would leave bible tracks on the seat of my car. I never read them. In fact, when I cleaned the car, they were thrown away with everything else. Many times she told me all I had to do to be saved was accept Jesus Christ as my Lord and Savior. I thought if she said that one more time, I was going to scream. Well, here I am, and through the grace of God, I have been delivered and couldn't be more grateful. This reminds me of a quote I heard, (Author unknown) "You can't give someone a gift they aren't ready to receive, but never underestimate the power of planting the seed!"

I recall the first time I picked up a bible years ago. I was flipping through the pages, full of curiosity, and decided to read the book of Revelation first. To say I found it terrifying is putting it mildly! For some time after, when reading the Bible was suggested, I thought to myself, "No thank you, I think I'll pass on that!" When I finally shared this with others, they lovingly encouraged me that if I started in the beginning, my fear would be replaced with hope! I will be forever grateful for that!

When Christ walked the earth, he gave us a road map (or what we can refer to as a GPS!) so we know how to follow him until we reach our final destination, forever in his presence.

In order to truly know God, Bible study is our best resource. Learning about who God is, by joining with others in the study of his Word, helps us all to have a better understanding, and it deepens our faith, and we grow together as the children of his kingdom.

Once again, I believe it's very important for all of us to remember that God never promised life would be easy! We often forget this when we are going through difficult times. Life happens, and sadness can prevail. We find ourselves losing our loved ones and feeling the intense pain of our loss. We may find our loved ones or ourselves dealing with serious health issues. Many things can happen in our lives to temporarily take away our joy and bring back our fears. How will life go on without those we love? Life brings unexpected changes, and we can feel all alone in our grief.

If we can keep in mind that although we can't prevent these things from happening, we are never alone. God is always with us. His loving Spirit will guide us if we ask for his intercession. Our trust in him carries us through the most difficult and darkest times. He places people in our lives to encourage us, or just sit quietly with us when the storms of life leave us feeling overwhelmed and physically or emotionally exhausted.

When we receive a smile from a total stranger when we are low in patience, feeling grumpy, or just feeling stressed, I believe that is Christ revealing his Spirit to us through others. We long to see him, and we don't realize how often we do! We see him through the love and compassion of others. This is truly amazing and fills us with hope and joy when we become aware of it!

If we choose to separate ourselves from God, then we will lose hope. This Scripture verse is uplifting to the soul and speaks of hope.

Psalm 62:5-6

6 For my hope is from Him. He alone is my rock and my salvation, my fortress; I shall not be shaken.

Chapter 11

When we experience things firsthand and realize there is a daily solution to our problems, it brings a deep sense of gratitude. It also fills a void in our souls and brings calm to our minds, and fills that void with hope. Through hope, we find our joy in Christ.

It is a blessing to share our life's challenges and struggles with others. We have been blessed so that we may be a blessing to others.

Some of us may have already realized the importance of being open and honest about our fears. Sometimes we may continue to struggle. Life isn't always smooth sailing. If life were perfect, we wouldn't be able to experience gratitude. We would be more likely to take life for granted. We would start making assumptions that life is always without trials and tribulations When we are struggling with life on life's terms there is no shame or judgement in that. One of the most reassuring and freeing messages to us in Scripture is found in **Romans 8**.

Life in the Spirit

Romans 8:1-4

> *8 There is therefore now no condemnation for those who are in Christ Jesus. For the law of the Spirit of life has set you free in Christ Jesus from the law of sin and death God has done what the law, weakened by the flesh, could not do. By sending his own Son in the likeness of sinful flesh and for sin, he condemned sin in the flesh, 4 in order that the righteous requirement of the law might be fulfilled in us, who walk not according to the flesh but according to the Spirit.*

What a reassuring promise found in this verse! When we are following Jesus, nothing or no one can condemn us! He has already paid the price for our sins, sealed by his blood shed on Calvary. What a glorious truth. The love that binds us to him in the unity of his Holy Spirit.

Another fear is that God may look upon us differently if we feel doubtful or are having trouble coping. When we calm our minds and seek His Spirit, He helps us to change our thoughts, and he blesses us with his guidance. Fear fails to exist when we are filled with His Holy Spirit. We feel his deep love for us. His love brings us the reassuring calmness that no matter what happens, He is always in control. We don't know what our future holds, but we can rest assured knowing it is he who holds our future.

Acceptance plays a crucial role in our faith journey. In our own humanness, We can make it difficult. We can quickly forget and end up creating our own problems. Instead of immediately seeking God's help, we can make things worse and start trying to deal with life on our own. Then we can find ourselves feeling hopeless and lost.

Holding on to our hope in Christ helps us survive the toughest of times. Sometimes hope is the very thing that carries us through the darkest moments in life. These difficult times can be our pathway to building a stronger foundation for our faith and childlike trust. I believe in our darkest, most difficult times, the nurturing, loving Spirit of God is closest to us.

We often pray desperately for a miracle when life doesn't go as planned. Amidst the struggles of life, we are surrounded by miracles. Life is a miracle in itself! The birth of a new life is evidence of the miracles God has created for us to witness, rejoice in, and bring us pure joy and happiness. All of his creations in the universe are evidence of his Supreme power to do all things.

In one of the parables in Scripture, Christ had performed a miracle, and his apostles questioned him. Why did they not have the same ability that he had to perform miracles?

His answer to them is found in **MATTHEW 17:20**

20 He said to them, "Because of your little faith. For truly, I say to you, if you have faith like a grain of mustard seed, you will say to this mountain, 'Move from here to there,' and it will move, and nothing will be impossible for you.

God is not saying that we alone have the power to literally move mountains. But through our faith in him, he blesses us with the courage to conquer our fears. Sometimes it can feel like we are trying to conquer a mountain ourselves when we are self-reliant instead of God-reliant.

One of the frequently used acronyms for fear is "Face everything and recover" or "Fear everything and run." We can run like Forest Gump as fast as our legs will carry us, or we can seek the faith of a mustard seed. It gives us awareness when we need to slow down. It provides us with the trust that God will carry our burdens for us.

Like many things in life, winning the battle with fear requires effort and trust. No matter how big or small our fears, nothing is too insignificant or difficult for God to handle! He created our vast, magnificent universe so he can surely calm the anxiety and fears of his children.

For you brave souls who have no fear, you may find it helpful to keep that in mind. We may feel strong in our faith, but we are not immune to the things that could lead us back to our old way of thinking, and our fears could resurface. To keep our faith alive, we have to be willing to search within ourselves so that we can find which component of our faith is missing.

Chapter 12

A key component of fear is courage. We are not born with an innate courage or natural instinct to be courageously heroic. Left to our own devices, we are defenseless against our human emotions when our minds are being fed by our own self- will. We may have the illusion of courage. We can instinctively respond to a dangerous situation, then later come to the realization that we reacted without considering the risk we took could have resulted in unanticipated consequences.

This is not to imply that we live in a world of thoughtless risk takers. There are people who have developed a sense of courage through hours of training to put their lives at risk to save the lives of others. Going into a burning building to rescue those who are trapped is only one example of this type of courage.

Awareness is a key element in our faith journey. It reminds us of what changes we need to make so we can lead a more God-centered, courageous life which brings Glory and Praise to His Name.

Humility is another component of our faith. The act of selfless courage didn't evolve from our human instincts. It came from the ultimate Divine courage of Jesus Christ, our Lord and Savior. The realization of his love for mankind brings humility beyond measure.

Letting go of our will and putting our trust in him can put our minds at ease. We find the soulful peace that our hearts and minds desire. We no longer have to walk through life searching for courage and feeling lost or defeated!

Trust begins within ourselves but is a lifelong process of continually seeking God's help. Through his grace, our trust in him, and our patience and humility, there is a solution to our life struggles.

Acceptance is another important element of our faith. Since we don't always know God's plans for us, acceptance can be difficult! When we reach out to him, asking him to help us except his will, and inviting him to touch us with His Spirit, it helps to remove our uncertainties and negative thoughts so we can feel the peace that will keep us in harmony with him. It redefines true happiness and not temporary happiness based on the material, superficial things of this world.

Knowing that he is not an unreachable God allows us to rejoice in his Spirit and pass on his love and light to others.

When we seek His Spirit, our doubts and struggles are no longer our own to bear. The turbulent storms of life are in his hands. When we become willing to surrender to his protection and care, we become one with him in the unity of his Holy Spirit.

Through him, we find the courage to face each day, and the burdens we carried in the past are no longer ours to carry! We find freedom through his infinite mercy and love.

The joy that trusts in God brings, changes us in such a profound way that we look at life through glimpses of our Creator's eyes, and our fears are placed safely in his hands.

When we become self-reliant and not God-reliant, life starts becoming more difficult, and it can rob us of the joy God has in store for us. I have learned that it's part of life to experience these growing pains. Growing in faith brings gratitude, and we become more aware of how desperately we need him to give us the strength to stand firm in our faith.

Chapter 13

Now that we have brought to light some of the most common fears, we have found our pathway to courage through faith. We find victory through Jesus Christ.

Will our faith save us from ourselves? In our human state, will every fear we have acknowledged be gone forever? Fear can appear when we least expect it. Building our own trusting relationship with God is always our best defense.

There are some things in life that we don't identify with or immediately recognize as fear. An example, if we suspect our spouse is being unfaithful, that fear can result in anger and jealousy. When our fears result in sin, it separates us from God. When we humbly turn to Him for forgiveness followed by repentance, this brings us back into the light of his grace, and we continue to seek His Spirit to guide us, and fill our hearts with the peace that only he can bring. When we are living according to God's will and have humbly surrendered to him, we continue to grow and build strength in our relationship with him.

When we are in a love relationship with others, if we are not fully present and putting effort into keeping that relationship alive, it becomes stagnant, and we grow apart.

The relationship we have with our Creator is the most sacred and important relationship we will ever have. We have to actively participate in our relationship with him. Everything we do to nurture our faith in him draws us closer to him and brings us his peace.

There are times in life when we will still find ourselves living in the flesh. We are not filled with God's Spirit every waking moment of our lives. If we were, we would be perfect and would not be sinners! The constant desire to be filled with his Spirit helps us not to get lost in self. We need him as much as we need the air to breathe!

When we are willing to be vigilant in our personal relationship with God, He blesses us and prepares us for life's struggles. The more time we spend seeking God's Spirit, the more joy we will experience. Pure joy in itself brings glory to God! He is not only our source of comfort but our source of joy.

God blessed us with happiness in the precious moments of this life. Through our hope in eternal life, forever in his presence, we will know everlasting joy! A joy that is ours forever as his faithful servants.

Chapter 14

Now that we have determined our fears, we can look at the positive sides of fear, which we refer to as "healthy" fears.

To fear separation from God is a healthy fear. It keeps us spiritually awake and gives us the desire to stay close to him.

Fear of complacency and laziness is also a healthy fear. This helps us to re-evaluate our lives and recognize what changes we need to make to fulfill our God-given purpose in life.

Fear of reverting to unhealthy habits, such as drug and alcohol abuse or intentionally isolating ourselves from the world, can be self-destructive and is recognized as a healthy fear. When we become mindful, we have the desire to change. As long as we turn the desire into willingness and put effort into making those necessary changes, we will reap the rewards that positive change brings.

Losing awareness of our need for God and one another is a healthy fear. Awareness that we are putting ourselves in a potentially dangerous situation and we avoid this from happening prevents our fears from becoming a reality. We can see the hand of God working in our lives when fear is averted.

Sharing with others that I have built a trusting relationship with has been a special blessing to me. Hopefully, we have all found a spiritual mentor. It can be a pastor, a priest, or a member of the clergy, but it can also be a trusted friend with whom we can be open and honest without holding on to fear of being judged. These special people were placed in our lives by God for a purpose. They help us along the way in our faith journey. Another example of how God makes His presence known to us through others.

When we are concerned about a family member or loved one, perhaps we fear they are making a poor choice that may put them in danger, we can express our concern, let them know that we love them, offer our support, and pray for them. We can't control the choices others make, nor should we try! Being aware of this saves us from worrying about these things.

Speaking from a parent's perspective, it's never easy. Especially when our children reach adulthood. We want what's best for them but they need to make their own decisions. Placing them in God's hands is easier said than done. Until we relinquish our will and surrender to God's will, we cannot know peace. We will find ourselves on an uphill battle trying to control things that God never intended for us to try to take control of in the first place.

When we surrender these situations to our loving God, we don't have to bear the burden of another person's choices. Developing a trusting relationship with God not only sets us free from our own fears but also the fears we have for those we love.

Surrendering our self-will and submission to God's will takes a heavy load off our shoulders! Sometimes we can try to carry some pretty heavy burdens! When we lay our burdens at his feet, we feel lighter, and he frees us from the undue suffering we can bring upon ourselves.

Chapter 15

We sometimes look at surrender in a negative light. Surrender is defined as giving in to the enemy or surrendering to an authority. Waving the white flag of surrender! In surrendering our will, we surrender to the "Divine" authority of our Sovereign God.

On several occasions, I have said I was turning a situation over to God. The next day, I was right back to square one, finding myself in God's way and trying to regain control. In almost every troubling situation, I have found I have very little or no control. This has proven to me that I'm going to be stuck in myself until I keep praying for acceptance of God's will.

If I am feeling discontent, it is usually because I am trying to run the ship, forgetting I am not the captain. Eventually, the ship is doomed to sink! When this happens, I am able to recognize I have been self-reliant and not God-reliant. I use this statement often because I ask myself this question as a reminder to myself!

Sometimes we create "road blocks" preventing us from moving forward. Praising God and thanking him through prayer, and asking him for his guidance, helps us to dismantle those "road blocks." Until we're willing to do that, we remain stuck! The analogy that comes to mind is like placing our feet in newly laid cement, and we're stuck there. Until we ask for help, we will remain stuck, unable to move forward.

I think many are hesitant to ask for help, perhaps because it can often be misinterpreted as a sign of weakness. Oftentimes, our ego and pride get in the way, and we're off and running, getting nowhere quickly!

Our human weakness can feel, at times, like we're running in a race and haven't taken the necessary measures to prepare. We're feeling tired, defeated, and wondering if we're going to make it. I think of Jesus at the end of that finish line. He's smiling, cheering us on, saying, "Run to Me! I love you! You can do all things through Me who strengthens you!"

Asking for help opens the door to honesty; it is not only humbling, but it also helps us to expose our true selves and acknowledge our imperfections without shame or guilt. This gives us the freedom to live a more courageous God-centered life.

We may stumble and fall many times, but with our faith in Christ, when we accept his salvation, through him we become victorious. He has already won the battle for us when he came back to earth to die for us so that we may have life and have it abundantly.

Through his guidance and divine intervention in our lives, we find the courage to let go of our fears and relinquish our weaknesses to him. It isn't a one-time effort. We are in constant need of God's help. When we submit to him, this draws us closer to him, and we find confidence through the intercession of his nurturing Spirit. This is the all-powerful, undefeated love of God.

Imagine for a moment the love that you feel for those who hold a special place in your heart. As strong as that love feels, it can't be compared to God's love. His love knows no boundaries. It's the never-ending love of our omnipotent God.

The desire to love others as he has loved us can arouse our passion to experience Godly love and not our imperfect human love. We make mistakes and can hurt those we love with our words and actions. When we reflect Godly love, we become whole, and we are complete in him!

Scripture shows us both his human side, when he became man, to show us how to live, forgive, and love. He died a courageous death for us, and he has given us his indestructible Spirit of love, He continues to reveal himself to us when we put him first in our lives. His love endures forever. He keeps his promise to never leave us stranded and feeling all alone when we follow him.

Deuteronomy 31:8

8: It is the LORD who goes before you; he will be with you and will never fail you or forsake you. So do not fear or be dismayed.

Chapter 16

Although we live in the midst of a broken world, our Father has not turned his back on us. We have created a mess on earth, constant chaos and discord, yet he offers us his forgiveness and mercy. He blesses us with his healing when we come to him in our own moments of brokenness. He meets us in our most difficult times when we call out to him with humility and desperation.

When life is going along smoothly, we can be easily distracted. Sometimes God is our plan B when he should always be our first choice above all else. We are far from perfect, so we don't always get it right. Our God is a patient God, but he is also a faithful and JUST God.

I have to pray every day for forgiveness for my sins and the strength to not repeat them. He forgives us and shows mercy on us in spite of our sins. Our unworthiness makes us humble before him as we praise and worship him. This verse speaks to us about our need to be humble before our merciful God.

1 Peter 5:6-7

6 Humble yourselves, therefore, under the mighty hand of God so that at the proper time he may exalt you,

7 casting all your anxieties on him, because he cares for you.

Humility is often found in the midst of turmoil. Being humble is a reaffirmation that everything that is done in the name of Jesus brings Glory to him. Without him, we would merely exist, and we would have no purpose in life. David expressed his humility in this beautiful verse in the Psalms.

Psalm 139:1-6

1 O Lord, you have searched me and known me!

2 You know when I sit down and when I rise up; you discern my thoughts from afar.

3 You search out my path, and my lying down, and are acquainted with all my ways.

4 Even before a word is on my tongue, behold, O Lord, you know it altogether.

5 You hem me in, behind and before, and lay your hand upon me.

6 Such knowledge is too wonderful for me; it is high; I cannot attain it.

Our human arrogance can indicate a lack of humility. How many times have we disagreed with someone, and we realized that being kind is more important than being right? If we don't remember this, then begins the battle of words. I have heard it said that we don't listen to others to "understand," we listen to "respond." Speaking for myself, I realized how true that has been.

Our ego is also fear-based. It can cancel out humility in a heartbeat. Our desire to be "right" can lead us to dangerous places where we are in a no-win situation.

Politics is a great example! Sometimes, when we engage in political conversations, it can be counterproductive and only lead to more hate and discord. I have definitely not always acted as a disciple of Christ when I have allowed myself to engage in political discussions. Through my own personal experience, through trial and error, I have learned that trying to convince others to see things my way has made me aware of my own desire to be right. I have to practice self-control, so my thoughts don't result in my words or reflect in my attitude. I know that condescending or unkind words do not come from the heart of Christ. Many times I have asked God to please help me keep the (imaginary) duct tape on my mouth! Politics can sometimes be the devil's playground, and I'm grateful to be cautious of this. Because I am a sinner, I am always in need of his mercy.

In a world where we are surrounded by evil, our God has prepared us to stand strong and without fear in the face of evil. He has given us his Word in the book of Ephesians. This tells us exactly how to expel evil and stand strong in faith. I have been trying to read this verse often and become very familiar with it. I think we can all agree that we are living in some very disturbing times. The devil doesn't hide anymore He has been released into the word and this verse prepares us to stand strong against his schemes to try and destroy our souls.

The Armor Of God

Ephesians 6:10-20

10 Finally, be strong in the Lord and in the strength of his might.

11 Put on the whole armor of God, that you may be able to stand against the schemes of the devil.

12 For we do not wrestle against flesh and blood, but against the rulers, against the authorities, against the cosmic powers over this present darkness, against the spiritual forces of evil in the heavenly places.

13 Therefore, take up the whole armor of God, that you may be able to withstand in the evil day, and having done all, to stand firm.

14 Stand therefore, having fastened on the belt of truth, and having put on the breastplate of righteousness,

15 and, as shoes for your feet, having put on the readiness given by the gospel of peace.

16 In all circumstances, take up the shield of faith, with which you can extinguish all the flaming darts of the evil one;

17 and take the helmet of salvation, and the sword of the Spirit, which is the word of God,

18 praying at all times in the Spirit, with all prayer and supplication. To that end, keep alert with all perseverance, making supplication for all the saints,

19 and also for me, that words may be given to me in opening my mouth boldly to proclaim the mystery of the gospel,

20 for which I am an ambassador in chains, that I may declare it boldly, as I ought to speak.

Chapter 17

Our hope in the Lord began with his mercy. He knew we needed a Savior. His decision to come to earth as his only Son changed everything for those who believe. His courage to endure unimaginable physical pain was fueled by perfect love and mercy. If we reflect on his mercy, it becomes our most humbling experience. This verse speaks of God's mercy to the people of Israel.

Isaiah 30:18

The Lord Will Be Gracious

18 Therefore, the Lord waits to be gracious to you, and therefore he exalts himself to show mercy to you. For the Lord is a God of justice; blessed are all those who wait for him.

Another verse that shows God's mercy can be found in Lamentations.

Lamentations 3:22-23

22 The steadfast love of the Lord never ceases; his mercies never come to an end

23 They are new every morning; great is your faithfulness.

24 *"The Lord is my portion," says my soul, "therefore I will hope in him."*

When we reflect on God's mercy and compassion, it leaves us in awe of him.

I try to stay focused on all the good that exists in the world. Our courage comes from God Himself, and I hope we all stay focused on His Almighty Power and Glory. Often, the evil in the world can draw the most attention and make the most noise. We need to stand firm in our faith to dismantle the power of the evil one. We don't have to fall prey to his evil ways if we stay connected to Jesus. God speaks truth and light, and the devil cowers in his presence.

To be loved so deeply by God amidst the chaos in the world and our sinful nature is evidence of His loving, forgiving nature. He is also a JUST God, and I hope we all will seek his forgiveness and mercy and turn away from the temptations that we are confronted with. We all need his guidance, mercy, and forgiveness.

If we visualize his suffering on the cross with his unfathomable pain and agony, I feel he was saying, "How much do I love you? With his arms outstretched wide, he was saying to all of us, "I love you this much!"

There is no other love that is more powerful and divinely courageous than the love of Christ.

Chapter 18

"The love chapter from 1 Corinthians

4-7!

4 Love is patient, love is kind. It does not envy, it does not boast, it is not proud.

5 It does not dishonor others, it is not self-seeking, it is not easily angered, it keeps no record of wrongs.

6. Love does not delight in evil but rejoices with the truth.

7 It always protects, always trusts, always hopes, always perseveres.

We often find ourselves falling short on patience! We can rush through life, trying to accomplish each task in a timely manner. It's easy to focus on what we are trying to accomplish, losing sight of those around us. This breeds impatience, and others can find themselves at the receiving end of our own frustration. Slowing down makes us more aware of our need to be lovingly patient with others and with ourselves!

Love is kindness. Kindness can be as natural as opening our eyes in the morning. It can also be as challenging as trying to walk a tightrope. Everything that Christ has commanded us to do requires love and often times putting the needs of others before our own. If we aren't spiritually in tune with Christ, we can fail miserably. Christ-like kindness requires more than just "politeness." It requires us to be aware so that the needs of others do not go unnoticed. This calls to mind the story of the Good Samaritan on the road to Jericho. Had he been self-absorbed, he would not have been aware of the man on the side of the road in need of help. Not only was he selfless in his kindness when he stopped to help the man, but he also paid for his stay at the Inn after he got him to safety. He didn't put a limit on how much kindness he was willing to give. Just like Christ didn't put a limit on how much torture he was willing to endure so that we could be forgiven.

Love does not envy. This isn't easy, especially when the ball of self-pity starts rolling! Loving others requires us to surrender our self-pity and learn to be accepting of others' good fortune, which is another form of Godly love. When I count my blessings by being truly grateful to God and thanking him, this releases the temptation to be envious of others.

Love does not boast. As a friend once suggested, "Do random acts of kindness and don't get caught." If I'm expecting a drum roll for doing an act of kindness, then I'm not reflecting Godly love. Avoiding the temptation to boast requires humility. In Ephesians, God instructs us not to boast.

Ephesian 2:8-9

8 For by grace you have been saved through faith. And this is not your own doing; it is the gift of God,

9 not a result of works, so that no one may boast.

Love is not proud. I think there is a big difference in being proud of our accomplishments and the accomplishments of others, when pride stems from awareness that all things good are a result of God's grace. "Stand alone pride" is running on our own self-will and crediting ourselves instead of acknowledging that God is the source of all that is good in our lives.

Love does not dishonor others. Dishonoring others can be done in many ways. Trying to bring others down in order to make ourselves feel better is a way we can dishonor others. Gossip or unloving reference to others dishonors them. Trying to get others to choose by taking sides in a conflict dishonors both people in a relationship. If we honor God above all else, then we are less likely to dishonor others.

Love is not self-seeking. Love sometimes requires us to put the needs of others ahead of our own needs. Self-seeking dishonors God because we are not praising him above all else. We are taking credit for our choices when our choices are made alone by not trusting God above all else. This can also arise from our human pride and arrogance. This blocks us from God's grace and causes us to sin against him. This can distance us from him and cause us to fail to love one another.

Love is not easily angered. Anger is one of the most dangerous of all emotions. We all get angry, or we wouldn't be human. Jesus was angry in the temple because others were dishonoring his Heavenly Father's house. It is holding on to the anger that is dangerous to ourselves and causes us to be unloving to others. Being too quick to anger means to me that I have unresolved issues that have not been dealt with. Until I look at what role I have played in any situation and assume responsibility for my part, I can't be a good example of Christ-like love. Being slow to anger shows self-control, which is a form of love and obedience to God.

Love keeps no record of wrongs. I'm sure there are some of us, especially couples, who can relate to this! We have a tendency to remind one another of past transgressions. I remember being upset with my husband and telling a friend I was not going to apologize because I had apologized the last time! She reminded me that no one was counting or keeping score. A great reminder that I was being the very opposite of loving. When God was asked how many times we should forgive, his response was clear. 77 times 7. In other words, we keep on forgiving as many times as we need to forgive. "Forgiving someone who hurt us doesn't mean we have to resume an unhealthy relationship with them, but we do have to find in our hearts a way to forgive them. If we aren't forgiving and we're keeping score, we are not honoring our love for Christ and one another.

Love does not delight in evil. The things in our lives that interfere with God's commandments, resulting in sin, cause evil actions. It intentionally causes verbal or physical harm to others and does not bring praise, honor, and glory to God. These things are the exact opposite of love.

Trying to justify our sins comes from Satan and his army of darkness. Only pure and Godly love can defeat evil and shine the light of love, which destroys the devil's schemes. Being fully clothed in the body armor of Christ, rejoices in His Glory and the evil one will flee. The love of God, when reflected in our words and actions, will always outshine the dark forces of evil. Love will always prevail! Every selfless act of love comes from the heart of God when he speaks through us. God is love, which is the most powerful and brightest light in the universe!

Chapter 19

I hope that reading this book has brought you peace, comfort, and strength in God's Word. You are deeply loved and cherished by our God!

Always remember that he knows your every thought, and he knows your doubts and fears before you even express them in your prayers. You and I were created in his image by the perfection of his hands. Being a part of his creations makes us all loved equally by our all-powerful Creator of the Universe.

Your life is important to him. You may feel you are just a speck in the universe to yourself and others, but to God you are each important, special and perfectly loved.

Your purpose in life may be to simply show compassion and love to others through kindness.

Perhaps God created you to minister the gospel to others as a leader and teacher. Whatever your purpose is, it is never unattainable in his eyes. It was perfectly planned since before you were created.

When you're feeling like you're low in faith, remember that it is in those moments of uncertainty that your faith can be rejuvenated and will actually become stronger. It may not feel that way when you're going through difficult times. I pray that you never grow tired of pursuing Gods purpose for you.

If you look back on times in life when you felt distraught and felt like giving up, those were the times the Spirit of God was there watching over you and blessing you. He wants you to find the inner peace that comes to you through him. Once you find that peace, he wants all of us to be his disciples and lead others to him.

He heals your pain and watches over you. God won't ever give up on you, so keep the faith and never allow yourselves to lose sight of him and his unconditional love, forgiveness and mercy.

May the peace and love of Christ be with you always. Through his grace and our faith in him, may he fill us with his Spirit, so we may all be "Divinely Courageous."

*****

The following chapters are testimonies from friends who have graciously accepted my invitation to share their personal faith testimonies of how they have overcome fear with relentless faith and courage.

Part 2.
Powerful Testimonies With Relentless Faith and Miraculous Healing

Chapter 20

Cory's Testimony

Cory is 33 years old. He is a sports enthusiast and an avid fan of the Cleveland sports teams, especially the Cleveland Guardians and the Browns! He also enjoys karaoke with family and friends, and is a pro wrestling enthusiast.

Cory comes from a very close-knit Christian family. His mom and dad have been his biggest supporters and prayer warriors. Cory has an older brother Will, who also has been both a brother and friend who has shown him love and support through the years.

Cory adores his two little nieces Adie and Ruby who fondly refer to him as "Funcle Cory!" They have brought much love and happiness to his life. His eyes lit up and his fondness for them reflected in his smile when he talked about how much he enjoys spending time with them.

When Cory was 5 years old, his parents had some health concerns for him and took him to their family Doctor. Medical testing determined he had Alport Syndrome, which also impacted his hearing and vision. Alport Syndrome is a rare hereditary disease that not only effected his hearing and vision but causes inflammation of the kidneys and eventually leads to renal failure.

Cory was then referred to a Nephrologist and he and his parents were off to Pittsburgh for a consultation.

Through his elementary and high school years, even though Cory was a gifted student and was able to excel in his studies, at times he felt detached from his friends and classmates.

Cory also has Autism/ Asperger's so it was difficult for him to feel like he fit in so he could have the feeling of "normalcy" that his fellow classmates had.

Cory's mom and dad raised him with faith and unconditional love. Even though his parents had enrolled him in a Christian school he had mixed emotions. Cory was a believer, yet he had a lot of questions during that time, that prevented him from having a close spiritual connection to God.

Through high school Cory's lab work became worse and by his 2nd year in college he had no other option than to drop out of school.

He and his mom and dad got the devastating news that it was finally happening. The news that you can't ever truly prepare for. Cory had gone into renal failure. it was an extremely difficult time for the rest of his family as well. It was now crucial for him to start kidney dialysis and for others to be evaluated to be a possible donor.

Since Cory was in complete kidney failure he needed to begin Peritoneal dialysis immediately. He was given a dialysis machine for use at home so he could receive his treatments daily. It was a frustrating time, especially for his mom, having the responsibility of making sure he was getting his treatments properly, so his kidneys would continue to function to keep him alive. This daily occurrence lasted for 19 long months! Although it took quite a toll on his family, the love they shared never wavered.

Cory's parents were praying their way through this extremely stressful time and reaching out to others asking them to pray for their son.

One particular night, Cory's mom, Mary, prayed all night and when she woke up, the idea came to her to start the Facebook page "You Only Need One" to help Cory and others in need of a kidney transplant. She knew this was a sign from God! Word spread quickly and many were praying all over the world for Cory, including Mary's friend Clare in Ireland.

Cory was placed on medication to help keep him alive. His dad also shares his enthusiasm for sports with a special interest in wrestling. They often spend father-son time, enjoying sports events together.

Cory's dad works in a local fitness center. Rob, a friend of Cory's dad, is also a wrestling fan. When Rob learned of Cory's dire need for a donor, he didn't hesitate to offer to donate his kidney. The family received an email from Rob. In the subject field of the email, they found the word "HOPE."

In May 2014, when Cory was only 21 years old, He and Rob formed a special lifelong bond. The transplant finally took place, and the anti-rejection medication was working, and Cory's body was accepting his new kidney.

In May 2026, it will be 12 years since Rob gave Cory his kidney. He and Rob make time to celebrate every year. Cory celebrates his gratitude to Rob for his love and willingness to give him a kidney to save his life.

God's timing is perfect, and Cory's gratitude opened the door to a spiritual awakening and deep gratitude to God for giving him another chance at life. Cory started believing in miracles, especially when he realized getting his life back was his own special miracle. A gift from God.

He started attending church again and became active with other Christians in a Bible study. Cory and his family's gratitude is beyond measure!

Cory's faith story did not end there!

Being a kidney recipient put Cory at high risk for infectious disease. His immune system was suppressed by the transplant medications.

In January of 2021, he wasn't feeling well. Despite being fully vaccinated, he was diagnosed with COVID. His symptoms were getting worse. He was showing no signs of improvement. He began struggling to breathe, and it was necessary for him to be placed on oxygen. He became so weak that he needed the assistance of a wheelchair since his body was continuing to become weaker, and his temperature was rising.

Cory had to be taken to the hospital by ambulance, and his condition became critical. Cory's mom and dad were living every parent's worst nightmare.

In the ICU, Cory had to be placed on a feeding tube, oxygen, and a breathing tube. After the ventilator, his lung collapsed, and he needed to have chest tubes inserted.

The Doctor gave Cory's dad a very grim assessment of Cory's condition. They just weren't sure that Cory's body could survive the stress of his critical condition.

His parents reached out again to prayer warriors everywhere! His dad cried out to God. "Jesus, Son of God, have mercy on my son."

One of Cory's friends started a hashtag #FightCoryFight! Prayer warriors everywhere were praying for him.

Cory has no memory of what took place in the weeks to follow. The only thing he was able to remember was having horrible nightmares.

His parents told him later that their Pastor also prayed over him in his hospital bed.

Cory shared with me that he believes God spared his life again for a reason. There is more God wants him to do. He has a passion for Christ, and he wants to share his passion with others. He has returned to school to complete his education.

I was honored and blessed to have Cory be so willing to share his faith and share his love for Christ with me and all who are blessed to hear his testimony. It is truly a reflection of faith, love, and his parents never giving up hope in the most desperate of times!

Cory is now spreading the love of Christ by hosting a Radio broadcast sharing Christian music on his university campus. Cory is fulfilling his desire to spread the love of Christ.

*****

May the peace of Christ continue to bless you, Cory, your family, your loving friend and donor Rob, and all you hold close at heart.

Chapter 21

Maura's Testimony

Maura is a former co-worker. She is a devoted wife with a loving husband. She is a very blessed mother to three children and a grandmother to nine. Her love for her family was obvious in her voice as she mentioned each member of her family and called them by name. Her family is her cherished treasure and the loves of her life.

When she was very young, she accepted Jesus into her life. As she looked back on that time in life, she realized that although he never abandoned her, she was still trying to manage life on her own. It felt as though she was always driving the car, and she had placed Jesus in the back seat.

Maura married in her twenties and thought she had met the man she would spend the rest of her life with. As time passed, her hope faded when her husband became physically abusive. The first time her husband became physically abusive with their children, there was no doubt in her mind that his abuse would no longer be tolerated, and the marriage ended in divorce.

Three years later, Maura met her second husband. Once again, she felt confident that this marriage would last forever. As time passed, some problems developed that tore them apart. She had to assume the role of both mom and dad since her husband was rarely home. She realized that his religious beliefs, which he was very silent about and didn't like to discuss, were very different than her own. She did try to get a better understanding of his faith and attended his place of worship. She tried participating in some of his church's functions, encouraging others to believe as they did.

Maura's soul was not at rest, and she knew she could never share the same beliefs. She realized that her heart belonged to Jesus and she would never walk away from her Christian faith. Since she was a Christian, she knew she had to find it in her heart to forgive him. Regardless, the marriage had become toxic and ended in divorce.

In 1996, Maura met David, who was also a Christian. They met at a divorce workshop at Grace Church. David invited Maura to go bowling and out to dinner. They spent the remainder of their date driving around, enjoying one another's company, and getting to know each other. After some time had passed, they decided to take a break for a while and sort out their feelings. They wanted to be sure. A mutual friend knew they loved one another. There was an altar call at church, and their friend joined both Maura and David's hands together, and they not only recommitted to Jesus but to one another. They were married in 1997 and have enjoyed 29 years of love and devotion to Jesus and to one another.

In 2020, Maura began having some health issues that were, at times, baffling to both her and her doctor. She started to experience heart palpitations. The episodes were sporadic, and her Dr. felt this racing heart problem was thyroid-related, so her medications were adjusted.

In June of 2023, the heart palpitations began to become more frequent. They became so troublesome that they were waking her up from a sound sleep. She went to the ER and was admitted to the hospital, and was told she had tachycardia AFIB.

By June 22nd, she found herself back in the ER again. To add to the AFIB, she had pain in her jaw that radiated down her arm. As all of these different heart issues continued to happen, Maura placed her trust in Jesus. He was her rock, and she had the confidence of knowing that, regardless of what happened next, Jesus was there with her in spirit, and she continued to rely on him, and she knew he would carry her through!

She remained in the hospital for an additional 5 days, and the doctors continued to run tests. None of these tests indicated she had a rare combination of heart problems. Maura requested an ablation, a procedure to treat her tachycardia. She didn't want to spend the rest of her life on medication. The ER Doctor recommended a heart catheterization to rule out any repercussions prior to the ablation. A cardiologist was consulted.

Maura turned again to Jesus, praying for his guidance. She felt peace in her heart and she felt that God's answer was yes. She proceeded to have the procedure.

She will always be grateful for God's guidance that helped her make her decision.

Unfortunately, she needed to have stents due to her hereditary condition of coronary heart disease. Had she not prayed and placed her trust in Christ, the outcome could have led to a stroke or massive heart attack. Maura put her faith and trust in God in action, and the result was truly miraculous!

In 2020, Maura began to devote herself to helping others through the Stephen Ministries. She wanted to be the feet of Jesus. Stephen Ministries is located all over the US, Canada, and many other countries throughout the world. Their mission is to reach out to others to share the light of Christ. Millions of people have been brought to Christ through very difficult circumstances, ranging from addiction to divorce, to comfort for the grieving.

In 2021, Maura became a teacher and a leader. She has continued on in her service to Stephen Ministries and has remained a grateful follower of Jesus, helping many to know the Lord and find peace and happiness in their faith journey.

*****

A special thank you, Maura, for your willingness to share your faith- filled testimony and continuing to serve as the feet of Jesus! May God continue to bless you as you lead others into his Kingdom.

Chapter 22

Heidi' H's Testimony Written by Heidi my friend in recovery.

The only woman I knew as a mother, my grandmother, died in 1999. It was one of the darkest, most depressing times of my life. I didn't know if my many years of sobriety were strong enough for this. I kept thinking to myself, "If only we had more time."

"Did I say everything I wanted to say? Did she know how much she was so very loved?"

I couldn't go to church without crying. Every time I tried to sing a church hymn, I couldn't. I was unable to hold back the tears. I experienced the same sadness at work. Before I went to bed, or before I did anything. I just kept telling myself I can't give up. I can't give in to any of the pain or anguish that I was feeling. So I got up every day, and I tried to just breathe, any try to get through one day at a time. One night, the pain seemed unbearable. I felt like I needed help.

I called out to God, and I begged for more help than I think I've ever asked him for. I told God about my pain and suffering and that I needed him to help me. I asked for a divine intervention.

I know you're not supposed to test God, but I needed her. So I asked him to send her to me. I didn't have to keep her, I just needed a moment. I prayed about that hard and often. Now, some may say it was a dream, or something made up in my head. But I know the truth.

When I went to bed that night, in my sleep, she came to me. I saw her, held her, smelled her scent, and I talked to her. I cried, and I held her so tight. I told her over and over how much I loved her. I remember she cried too and told me how much she loved me. We briefly broke apart and looked at each other. Again, the tears would start all over again, and we held one another so tight. It lasted through the whole night until I woke up. When I woke up, my face and pillow were soaked with tears.

God does answer prayers. He knows what you need and when you need it. I thank Him all the time because having her near doesn't ease all pain, but I'm able to go on.

Because of what I've been through, I'm able to help others who suffer from the pain of grief and addiction.

I'm so grateful to God for bringing her to me, maintaining a sober life, and all of my many blessings.

*****

Thank you, Heidi, for reminding all of us that God answers prayers, even the ones that seem impossible. May God continue to bless you on your faith journey. I'm grateful to call you a friend in recovery!

Chapter 23

Debbie's Testimony

Debbie and I have shared a lifelong friendship. Her devotion to God and especially prayer has always been an inspiration to me. Many times through the years, we have shared laughter together, when she would declare she was arguing with God again! Some may see that as strange or disrespectful, but I have always seen her as a woman who has a close relationship with our Lord.

Debbie has raised two children. Her daughter Erika and her son Matt. Her children and grandchildren are the loves of her life.

Life changed very quickly for Debbie when Matt was diagnosed with cancer. She didn't waste time rounding up all the prayer warriors, asking them to pray for her son. A mother on a mission, she was willing to move heaven and earth to pray for God's divine intervention for Matt.

Matt went into remission but still has challenges ahead to prevent a cancer recurrence. She continues to plead with God and his power to heal on Matt's behalf. As difficult as it has been for Matt, she has not and never will stop praying for him. A bond between a mother and child is like no other!

On Father's Day in 2021, Debbie received a call from Minnesota, where her daughter had transferred for a job as CEO in retail sales. She was employed by a large company that extended from the US to Europe.

It was the beginning of a nightmare that has changed Debbie forever. The Doctor told Debbie that Erika was non-responsive and in a coma. Debbie needed to get there as soon as she could, so she booked a flight and headed to Minnesota.

I missed a call from Debbie that Sunday morning. When I reached Debbie, she said, "It's Erika, and please just pray."

She was beside herself, and I couldn't imagine the fear and worry she experienced on her flight to the hospital. To say this was devastating is an understatement. There are simply no words to describe a Mother's heartache. The shock was unimaginable.

Erika had been home that day. She was actually working out in her in-home gym when she collapsed. Prior to that, she was in perfect health.

When she arrived at the hospital, Debbie received news that no parent wants to hear. It was unlikely that Erika would ever recover from the coma. Debbie's heart was shattered.

The team of Doctors suspected that Erika had an extremely rare reaction to one of the Covid vaccines. Erika had received. She never regained consciousness.

In the wee hours during the stillness of the night, Debbie posted a video to her family and friends as she walked down the hall to say her final goodbye to Erika. She didn't want to take that walk alone. She knew God had not abandoned her, but it was the worst emotional pain she was ever faced with.

Erika's organs that were not affected were donated so others may live. An act of love among the unbearable grief.

The days that followed were a blur. The shock, the tears, and the concern for Erika's two young children and her husband were unfathomable. She cried out to God. Why God would you take my child?!

During the Mass to celebrate Erika's life, she felt like she was having a bad dream. Please, God, help me to understand why you would take my baby girl.

Erika was 44 years old and had her whole life ahead of her. They had a close mother/daughter bond. They could weather any storm together.

Despite her anger at God and the horrific emotional pain, she knew deep down that Erika was in God's arms. She shared with me that she was barely reaching for God's hand and wasn't sure she could hold on.

Was God testing her faith? If he was, she wasn't sure if she could pass the test. Even though she was barely hanging in there, Debbie had no clue how much she has inspired those who know and love her.

Debbie's mom suffers from Alzheimer's. Even though she was there for Erika's funeral, her failing memory made it difficult to communicate with her. Debbie needed her mom's support as she began the grief process, but her mom's mental state made that close to impossible.

The following summer, Debbie and her family celebrated Erika's life with the release of butterflies. There was a slight breeze that day and a feeling of peace and serenity. I felt honored to be a small part of this celebration of Erika's life.

As heartbreaking as it is, Debbie knows and believes her daughter is with the Lord. She has felt Erika's strong presence very near her. A peaceful feeling that Erika is walking with her through her grief.

Debbie has good days and difficult days. She has faith to believe that someday she will see her daughter again. She feels Erika's is asking God to send his angels to comfort her when the grief seems unbearable.

*****

Thank you for our many years of friendship Debbie, and your willingness to share your faith. Occasionally even laughter through the tears, knowing that Erika's spirit is close by. May your faith bring you peace and strength. I pray God will comfort you. Just like in foot prints, it is now that he carries you!

Part 3.
Precious Moments With Jesus

Inspired by his Word in Scripture

My Dearest Child

As you awake this morning, know that I am nearby. Begin your day by talking to Me and delight in Me as I help you to prepare for this day. This new day is my special gift to you. Remember to pause during this day and think of my love for you. When you are feeling upset and troubled, remember to look towards Me. I will change your heart. My love will bring you into my light and guide you away from the things that will harm you. I want you to rejoice in My Glory and bask in the Sunlight of My Spirit.

My Anxious Child

When your mind is racing with troubling thoughts, I will replace the chatter of your thoughts with My peace and strength. I will cast out all the noise! I will bless you with calm, and you will find comfort in Me. I am here with you, but you must remember to call out to Me. Your soul needs My Spirit to intercede for you. Focus on Me, my child, and avoid those things which disturb your mind and take you out of the realm of My Spirit.

My Precious Child

Your soul longs for Me. I am here with you when you seek my goodness. If you follow Me throughout your day, your eyes will be opened, and you will see My blessings with clarity. I will cast out confusion and doubt and shed My light upon you. When you walk with Me, you will know My heart and turn away from the ways of the world and find your joy in Me. I am your shield of armor, which protects you from harm. I will guide you and bless you with My Grace when you seek My face.

My Struggling Child

When life gets hard and you struggle to find inner peace, place your trust in Me. You will continue to struggle needlessly until you search your heart for Me. My Spirit is right here with you. Why do you wait? When you cry out to Me, I will help you. I will pour out My strength in you. I will bless you, and you will find the peace you long for. Never allow yourself to lose sight of Me. Always come quickly to Me when you are in distress.

My troubled child

When you turn away from Me, you cannot feel My forgiveness and mercy. You must turn away from the evil one. My love for you is steadfast and faithful. Turn away from your sins, and I will forgive you. I will rescue you, My child, and protect you from the grasp of My enemies. My Spirit of love in you cannot be defeated when your eyes are focused on Me.

My cherished Loved One

I know the sound of your heartbeat. Every breath you take is My gift to you. I watch over you as you sleep and as you open your eyes in the morning. I created you for My pleasure and glory. Feel my presence close to you, and I will walk with you. I will surround you with My gentle Spirit. I will go before you and prepare the path ahead. When you walk with Me, you will not stumble and fall.

My Beloved Child

Draw near to Me by spending time with Me. Read my Words to you in my Holy Scriptures. This will help you to know Me, Honor Me, and Glorify My Holy Name. When you long to know Me better, your love for Me will grow, and you will crave to know more about Me. Remember not to lean on your own understanding! Seek communion with others who desire to follow Me. I will bless your minds and hearts and fill you with My Divine Spirit of Truth.

My Precious Fearful Child

Rest your mind, and I will replace your fears with hope in Me. When you cry out to Me, I will calm your mind. You must trust that I will protect you from your fears. Do not let your thoughts separate you from Me. Pray to Me with Praise and Thanksgiving. Honor Me with your words and actions. I will take mercy on you and guide you out of the darkness into the light of My radiant presence.

My Loving Faithful Child

When you sing your songs of praise to Me, it brings Me joy, and I delight in you. When your passion for Me brings tears of joy to your eyes, I exalt you!. My Spirit joins with yours, and My perfect peace is with you. Continue to worship Me and praise Me above all else! I will pour My blessings upon you, and you will feel My joy in you. Do not be selfish with your joy in Me. Spread my love and your hope in Me with eagerness! Reach out to those who are suffering from the absence of My Presence. They are also my precious children.

My Distraught, Angry Child

When My Spirit comes to you, I bring peace and love. When your heart is filled with anger, you cannot feel the joy of My presence. Talk to Me about your anger. Tell me what is causing your rage. I already know your thoughts. I am a patient God, but you must release your anger to me so that I can help you. Be patient with others and with yourself. The sooner you let go of what is damaging to your soul, the sooner I can restore your mind, body, and spirit and make you whole again. Forgive yourself and ask for My forgiveness. Forgiving others will set you free. Be patient and let Me guide you back into My loving Spirit of Peace.

My Sad Depressed Child

I have promised to never leave you. I will hold you close to Me and help you come out of your darkness. I love you, my child. Ask me to watch over you, and you will never need to feel alone. I will walk beside you, and you will find your hope in Me. Do not let the evil one deceive you! Look around you for others who reflect my peace and happiness. My light will shine through them, to you. Ask Me to fill you with My Spirit of strength. You need Me to pull you out of your pit of darkness. Come to me, and I will heal you. I will not abandon you nor forsake you.

My Dear Grieving Child

I see every tear you shed. My heart longs to console you. Reach out to me in your pain. Find your refuge in Me and invite Me to walk with you as you mourn. Allow yourself to grieve, and I will carry you through your sorrow. Remember that life is temporary, but I have promised you eternal life, forever in My presence. Come follow Me, and I will bless you with My healing. Do not lose hope in Me through your time of grief. I am your Almighty God, who can restore you back to who I created you to be. Be patient in your trials. Trust in Me and remember My promise that someday there will be no more tears and sorrow. You will meet your loved ones in the place I have prepared for you.

My Precious Doubtful Child

I see how troubled and uncertain you are. You have much to learn about Me! Focus on the good in the world. This is where you will find Me. You will find my goodness and beauty in all that I have created. Do not fear, for I watch over you. Do not allow doubt to overcome you. Clear your thoughts of negativity. You will not find me in the chaos of the world. You will find me in the quietness of your mind. Keep searching for me. The evil in the world is not where My Spirit lives. Turn away from all that keeps you apart from me. I will bless you with my saving Grace, but you must seek my Spirit so I can fill your heart with love for Me, and you will find your faith in Me!

Part 4.
Additional Comforting Scriptures Verses Pertaining to Fear

Additional Scripture verses with reference to Fear or Fear Not Taken from NIV (New international version)

1 John 4:18

18 There is no fear in love. But perfect love drives out fear, because fear has to do with punishment. The one who fears is not made perfect in love.

Joshua 1:9

9 Have I not commanded you? Be strong and courageous. Do not be afraid; do not be discouraged, for the Lord your God will be with you wherever you go.

Psalm 23:4

4 Even though I walk through the valley of the shadow of death, I will fear no evil, for you are with me; your rod and your staff, they comfort me.

Psalm 34:4

4 I sought the Lord, and he answered me and delivered me from all my fears.

Psalm 27:1

1 The Lord is my light and my salvation; whom shall I fear? The Lord is the stronghold of my life; of whom shall I be afraid?

John 14:27

27 Peace I leave with you; my peace I give to you. Not as the world gives do I give to you. Let not your hearts be troubled, neither let them be afraid.

Psalm 56:3-4

3-4 When I am afraid, I put my trust in you. In God, whose word I praise, in God I trust; I shall not be afraid. What can flesh do to me?

Romans 8:38-39

38-39 For I am sure that neither death nor life, nor angels nor rulers, nor things present nor things to come, nor powers, nor height nor depth, nor anything else in all creation, will be able to separate us from the love of God in Christ Jesus our Lord.

1 Peter 5:6-7

6-7 Humble yourselves, therefore, under the mighty hand of God so that at the proper time he may exalt you, casting all your anxieties on him, because he cares for you.

Psalm 118:6

6 The Lord is on my side; I will not fear. What can man do to me?

Isaiah 43:1-3

1-3 But now thus says the Lord, he who created you, O Jacob, he who formed you, O Israel: "Fear not, for I have redeemed you; I have called you by name, you are mine. When you pass through the waters, I will be with you; and through the rivers, they shall not overwhelm you; when you walk through fire, you shall not be burned, and the flame shall not consume you, for I am the Lord your God, the Holy One of Israel, your Savior.

Hebrews 13:6

6 So we can confidently say, "The Lord is my helper; I will not fear; what can man do to me?"

Psalm 91:9-11

9-11 If you say, "The Lord is my refuge," and you make the Most High your dwelling, no harm will overtake you, no disaster will come near your tent, for he will command his angels concerning you to guard you in all your ways.

Isaiah 12:2

2 Behold, God is my salvation; I will trust, and will not be afraid; for the Lord God is my strength and my song, and he has become my salvation.

Isaiah 41:10

*10 So do not **fear**, for I am with you; do not be dismayed, for I am your God. I will strengthen you and help you; I will uphold you with my righteous right hand.*

Psalm 111:10

10 *The fear of the Lord is the beginning of wisdom; all those who practice it have a good understanding. His praise endures forever!*

Psalm 112:1

1 *Praise the Lord! Blessed is the man who fears the Lord, who greatly delights in his commandments!*

Psalm 31:19

19 *Oh, how abundant is your goodness, which you have stored up for those who fear you and worked for those who take refuge in you, in the sight of the children of mankind*

Psalm 25:14

14 *The friendship of the Lord is for those who fear him, and he makes known to them his covenant.*

2 Corinthians 7:1

1 *Since we have these promises, beloved, let us cleanse ourselves from every defilement of body and spirit, bringing holiness to completion in the fear of God.*

2 Timothy 1:7

7 *For the Spirit God gave us does not make us timid, but gives us power, love and self-discipline.*

www.ingramcontent.com/pod-product-compliance
Lightning Source LLC
Chambersburg PA
CBHW071456130726
47997CB00006B/2364